The Internet Candidate

The Internet Candidate

Stress Reduction through a New Kind of Political Force

Albert Childress

Amindro Corporation
Lexington, Massachusetts

Amindro Corporation
33 Liberty Avenue
Lexington, MA 02420
www.amindro.com

Printed in the United States of America.

Library of Congress Control Number: 2006939077

ISBN-13: 978-1-933136-02-8
ISBN-10: 1-933136-02-2

Contents

Contents.. v

Dedication..ix

Preface xi

1. Introduction 1

2. Stress in the Modern World............. 9

    Job 13

    Family 14

    Driving Drunk..............................16

    Poverty 17

    Mental Illness 17

    Racial Tension...............................18

    Crime...18

    Pets..19

Money 19

Health 20

Neighbors...................................... 20

Litigation 21

Fear... 21

Time 23

Cumulative Stress........................ 24

Culture of Rudeness...................... 25

Cycle of Stress 26

Safety Net.................................... 27

Coping... 28

Loss of Self-Reflection 28

Self-Actualization.......................... 29

Impact on Politics......................... 30

Passion for Politics....................... 31

3. Hurricane Katrina 33

Broader Message 34

Pitiful Response 36

4. Today's Broken Political System..... 39

Problems 40

The Reduction of Stress 41

The Power of the Internet............. 44

Choice of Candidates..................... 46

The Politics of Old 47

5. The Internet.............................51
    Politics Untouched.........................52
    A New Political Force 53
6. The Internet Candidate 57
    We the People..............................59
    Elections....................................61
    Candidates 64
7. The Stress Index..........................67
    Indices 68
    Measurements.............................69
8. The Future.................................71
    No More Two-Party System 72
    Online Communication..................73
    The Creation of Community..........73
    A Return of Passion 74
9. Action Items and Challenges...........75
    Action Items...............................76
    Challenges.................................77
10. Conclusion 79

Dedication

This book is dedicated to Ian and Anna, my wonderful children, in the hopes that our broken political system can be fixed before they are too old to benefit from the fix.

Albert Childress

Preface

This book is meant to provoke thought and produce political action. It explores the unfortunate reality of our world today and the hopeful possibility of positive change in the future.

Albert Childress

Chapter 1

Introduction

Our current political system is broken. It isn't addressing the needs of the people. Too many people are under too much stress in today's society. Politicians are beholden to the current system. They aren't like us and therefore can't truly represent us. We need to change politics in order to reduce stress. Our lives could then be more meaningful.

In this book, I make the case for improving our lives by using the Internet to bring politics back to us, the people. Our founding fathers set up a system of representative government. We need to respect that system. It is critical that we produce the best candidates to meet our needs. The political process needs an infusion of life and passion. We need to elect politicians who will make laws and policies to reduce the stresses in our lives.

The argument in this book is straightforward:

- The modern world is a stressful place, much more stressful than it has to be.

- The current two-party political system is broken. It produces candidates who can't, or won't, address the stresses of modern life.

- The time has come to use the Internet, which has yet to be tapped to its full potential in politics, as a vehicle of change to return government to the people.

- Our lack of proper representation makes today's politics a stress producer.

- The new kind of political force proposed in this book will make politics a mechanism for stress reduction, both directly and indirectly. The more input and control we have over candidate selection, the less stress we will feel in our political lives. Furthermore, as soon as we select candidates who formulate laws and policies designed to reduce stress, our stress levels will decline.

The new political force proposed in this book will allow positive changes to take place in politics:

- Our voices will be heard and our preferences known. We will elect candidates who represent us.

- The two-party system will fade away as we use the Internet to choose candidates. In today's political system, we vote for candidates who are presented to us by political parties. Going forward, we will take over that process for ourselves. We will control our political destiny.

- A new Stress Index will keep track of stress in society. This Stress Index can be used to evaluate whether laws and policies are reducing stress.

- In the future, voting, polling, community meetings, and political interactions will take place online. More effective communication will result.

- As we become represented by people like us, we will become more passionate about politics than we currently are. And isn't passionate involvement the goal of politics?

The Internet can shrink the world and make the national political process more local. We can choose more effective candidates, get rid of the two-party system, measure the stresses of modern life with a Stress Index, communicate better, participate in politics with renewed passion, and lead less stressful and more fulfilling lives. We're here for only a limited time, so we may as well make the journey as smooth as possible.

This book proposes a collective endeavor. We need to work together to produce the Internet Candidate, a candidate we select among ourselves for ourselves. Career politicians need not apply. Those who choose candidates and make deals in back rooms can stay in those back rooms while the rest of us improve politics for ourselves and our descendents.

Many changes are needed. We need to rid ourselves of the two-party system. We need to come up with a way to measure stress in society so that our leaders will be accountable for passing laws and policies that reduce stress. Those leaders who can't reduce our stress levels will be voted out of office in subsequent elections. We will bring communication and passion back to politics. Passion will come from renewed participation. Leaders will be responsive to us because they will be chosen from our ranks.

Ultimately, you will have to decide whether you want to try to achieve the goals of this book via the mechanisms suggested by this book. The world isn't as simple as it used to be, but we can work to reduce stress before it renders our lives devoid of meaning. It's time for a meaningful change in politics.

Let's bring politics back to us, the people. Let's hold our leaders accountable for reducing the stresses of modern life. Let's compete favorably with corporations and lobbying groups. Let's shape the world in our image.

The Internet has given us a new way to change politics for the better. The Internet has already changed how we gather information and buy goods and services. Now, it's time for the Internet to change how we participate in politics.

This book is designed to stimulate thought, provoke discussion, and promote action. In some ways, it is a self-help book, with the goal of helping you reduce stress in your life. For it to be effective, many of us will need to discard the helpless feelings we now harbor towards politics and embrace a more participatory style of political engagement. In other ways, this book is a political essay, with the goal of changing the political system to make it more responsive to our needs.

I ask that you read this book, digest its contents, and act in such a way that your needs are met. If this book resonates with you, I hope that you will take action by working with others to make our lives less stressful and more fulfilling.

Chapter 2

Stress in the Modern World

Let's be honest with each other. Living in America right now is stressful. Very stressful. And things don't seem to be improving.

You don't know me, so don't just take my word for it. Examine your own life. Look at your relationship with your spouse. Consider how hard it is for some of you even to find a spouse. Think about what it takes to raise your kids. Consider your job. Is it what you want to do? Do you feel stuck there? Do you even have a job?

A list of life's stressors could go on for pages and pages. Do you have any health problems? Financial problems? Is your neighbor's dog keeping you up at night? Is the air in your home making you sick? Have you ever been abused? Do you have time for yourself?

Living under stress requires a great deal of effort. In such a world, even little things that don't go smoothly impact us more than they ought to. Little stressors simply add up. I don't mean to sound petty, but do your shoes fit as comfortably as you want them to? Did you forget one item at the store and now have to make another trip there? Did you accidentally bounce a check, generating bank fees and creating the need to rebalance your checkbook? Small items like these, which shouldn't be hard to absorb, can seem overwhelming in a stressful world, a world in which we are already stretched too thin.

When we are under stress, we are not as friendly towards others as we should be. When we are not friendly towards others, we add to their stress and to our own. All of us have seen signs of this. The person at the table next to us snaps at the waiter or waitress. Drivers flip each other off. Parents fight at children's sporting events. Spouses go to bed not speaking to each other.

We have no exact measures of societal stress, so you'll have to be your own judge about how stressful the world is. If you are under stress and wish that some of it could be alleviated, please read on. If you don't feel the stresses of modern life, humor the rest of us and read on so that you can see how others live. Perhaps you're part of the problem and not part of the solution. Either way, read on.

Stress is all around and increasingly hard to avoid. But shouldn't we at least be able to participate in a political system that allows us to choose candidates who understand how stressful the world has become and who will take measures to reduce that stress? Today's two-party political system, a system that often picks political candidates who have never felt financial or emotional stress, is not one that is best designed to meet our stress-reduction needs.

You might be saying that stress is part of life. But, even so, can't we make things less stressful? Don't we want our lives to be easier? Can we really find our true selves in a world where the daily grind takes too much time and energy?

Our lives are limited in duration. Living under stress can't be what life is all about. As citizens of a free country, we have the power to shape our destiny. Let's figure out how to use that power to produce a less stressful existence.

It's not hard to make the point that the modern world is a stressful place. We can all point to things that are stressful.

But let's not move on just yet. Let's dig in a bit further to understand where we are.

The desire to live a less stressful existence is the key underpinning of the changes proposed in this book, so we can't gloss over stress. We have to confront it and understand what it is doing to us. We have to imagine the potential of a less stressful existence. Only then can we bring renewed passion to politics.

Job

Job stress is all too real. Bosses can be difficult to work for and colleagues difficult to work with. If you designed a stressful place, the daily grind of work and annual performance reviews would be part of the blueprints.

The time spent at work can exacerbate other areas of stress. The hours devoted to work result in less time available for family, friends, and self. Financial stress is often connected to a job. Fear of job loss guides negative thinking.

It's not that a job can't be a joyous thing. It can be. However, once we get stuck in a particular job, it becomes hard to leave. Why not elect political candidates who will make it easier for us to switch jobs?

And whoever said that a forty-hour work week should be the norm? How about thirty? What about vacation time? Corporations have shackled us with their perceptions of reasonable vacation time. With the Internet Candidate, who will be chosen by us and for us, we can decide how much vacation time is available to us.

Family

Although potentially one of the greatest sources of stress reduction, family can also be a significant cause of stress. Arguing with a spouse can be a daily event. Illnesses can be serious enough to require medical attention. Affairs are common, as is divorce. Children with learning or behavioral issues can create challenges. Caring for elderly parents is not unusual.

Family stresses may be unavoidable at some level, but we need to have laws and policies in place that allow us to deal with these problems directly, without the interference of other stressors. Granted, there are currently some laws and policies that allow for easier juggling of family needs and job demands, but those are just the start of what is needed.

We need laws and policies that will allow for a much better balance between work and family. If your child is sick and has to miss school, you shouldn't have to worry about possibly losing your job. The modern world has many people who are struggling to balance work with family.

Laws and policies need to be aligned with the modern world. What better way to achieve this alignment than to choose candidates who understand the stresses of the modern world and who are beholden to the people and not to corporate lobbyists?

Driving Drunk

Many of us have seen statistics about the number of families impacted by drunk drivers. Drunk drivers kill. However, the laws in place for driving drunk amount to little more than a slap on the wrist.

This unfortunate state of affairs results from the fact that so many current politicians have grown up in a world where people drive drunk. Some even drive drunk themselves. Going forward, we need to select candidates who will push for harsher laws against drunk driving and who will not worry about the impact of these stricter laws on the breweries of the world.

Poverty

As a wealthy country, we should be ashamed that so many are living in poverty. Although we rarely confront it, this background perception of how so many can live with so little in this land of plenty creates an undercurrent of stress.

Instead of watching politicians ponder how to reduce taxes on the wealthiest members of society, let's look at how to spend money intelligently to provide a safety net for those who need it. Selecting candidates who are like us will maximize our chances of living in a society with an appropriate safety net.

Mental Illness

There are fewer and fewer options for the mentally ill. We need to face the fact that something about our society is not working if so many are affected by mental illness. Could we increase the pay of people who work to help the mentally ill? Could we provide more alternatives for care and treatment? Let's work to improve matters.

Racial Tension

The United States should be proud that it has such a diverse population. Unfortunately, not everyone agrees with this sentiment. To be confronted with racial hostility is very stressful.

Crime

Think about how crime adds stress to our lives. We lock and double-check our doors. We buy alarms and guard dogs. We call the police if we see unusual people in our neighborhoods. We may wisely refuse to open our doors to strangers, but the stress we feel is real. If we choose candidates who understand that a safer world is a less stressful world, we are more likely to reduce some of the stressors in our society.

Pets

Pets used to be easier to own. Now, we live in closer quarters where pets can't roam as freely as they should. Also, we have added dangerous breeds to the mix. Today, anyone who comes across a dog has to move the other way. What kind of world is that?

Money

Who can argue with money as a source of stress? We toil in jobs to make more money. Marriages crumble because of disagreements over money. We worry about how to pay our current bills, how to save for retirement, and how to save for our children's education. People stay in undesirable jobs just to make money to pay for living expenses. This is a stressful way to live.

Health

The loss of good health can impact all areas of life, from our ability to work to our ability to interact effectively with family and friends. If other stressors such as a job prevent us from devoting the proper amount of time to health issues, then those health issues will be more burdensome than they should be.

Neighbors

Need I pursue this one? Let me just remind you that barking dogs, falling tree limbs, and misplaced fences can be a stressful part of our lives. Our neighborly interactions would be more civil if other areas of our life were less stressful.

Litigation

With its emphasis on resolving disputes through litigation, our society has led people to be wary of interacting fully with others or even helping those in need. It used to be that a person who collapsed in a restaurant could receive aid. Now, there is some hesitation about getting involved. This state of affairs is unfortunate.

Fear

Our lives today are filled with fear. Going to the dentist is scary for many. I overheard someone say that they are scared to go to the barber because they might get nicked and infected with some sort of disease. Being in the sun used to be fun. Now, it could lead to skin cancer. Your neighbor's green lawn might be nice to look at, but it could be sending pesticides your way. Sharing a cup of water with someone could make you sick. Even a tick is a scary thing.

We can't read the newspaper these days without learning that something else might be harmful. An environment of fear increases stress. Will this hamburger kill me? How about the new carpet in my office? Could my date have herpes or worse? And how will that roller coaster affect my brainstem? Will my property be damaged by an earthquake, heavy winds, falling tree branches, or a flood?

The list of fears is potentially endless. Terrorist threats after September 11, 2001, are near the top of list. Natural disasters after the tsunami of December 2004 and Hurricane Katrina of August 2005 are causing untold concern. News about the possible pandemic of avian flu is worrisome.

An earlier generation grew up with the constant threat of nuclear attack by the Soviet Union. A new generation is growing up with the threat of terrorist attacks.

The list of fears and threats could go on and on, and that is the point.

Time

Time is short. Multitasking is common. How many of us try to do several things at once so that we might be able to increase our free time? Free time, you ask. What free time?

And remember that almost everybody you interact with is under similar time constraints. What could be a relaxed interaction can become stressful because of someone else's time constraints. Busy lives spiral out of control. People rush through the day.

Time is too compressed and rushed. Technology is making us accessible at will (someone else's will, that is). Faxes, telephone calls, and e-mail can come in at any time of the day or night. Being reachable via e-mail and cell phones has some benefits, but we have little time left over for ourselves.

Cumulative Stress

Any one item of stress has a greater chance of being absorbed and dealt with if it is the only item of stress. However, that is rarely the case today. Our lives have become so stressful that we can't absorb more and more stress. That inability to absorb more stress is the impetus for this book. We should not have to go through life fully loaded with stress. If we are under too much stress, we can't live our lives effectively.

It is unlikely that we can get rid of all stress. But if we can get rid of some key sources of stress, we will be able to deal with the remaining areas of stress in a more palatable way.

Culture of Rudeness

Perhaps the results of today's stress overload can be seen in the culture of rudeness that has developed. Witness how strangers interact with each other on the highway. Watch how students behave towards teachers on field trips.

A big problem is that most of us are stretched too thin. Although we do the best we can to minimize stress, that may not be good enough. Starting and ending the day with a stress overload does not help.

All of us need to be part of a movement that forces our leaders to make laws and policies that reduce the stresses in our lives. The first step is to use the Internet to take charge of choosing political candidates who understand the stresses of modern life and who will work to reduce stress where possible.

Cycle of Stress

The basic building block for this book is stress reduction. The reduction of stress should motivate us to adopt the new brand of politics advocated in this book.

There is so much stress in the modern world that we run the risk of accepting it as a necessary component of society. Stress in the modern world is, in part, the product of having too little time available. Having too little time leaves no room for mistakes.

Stress is also the product of fears. It is the result of not having a safety net. At any given time, a health crisis or job loss could devastate your life and the lives of your family and friends.

Because we are under stress, we can't perform as well in our jobs as we would like. Our limited performance in our jobs then becomes a new source of stress. A vicious cycle of stress that begets more stress has begun. Marital discord is a cause of stress, but marital discord can also result from stress. Let's reduce stress all around and stop these vicious cycles.

Of course, things could be worse. Loving families, fulfilling jobs, and good health do exist. But even those who are not impacted by the greatest stressors would have a better life if the stress level of society came down a notch. The fewer stresses there are, the more fulfilling all of our interactions will be.

Safety Net

We need a safety net to reduce some of our stresses. Safety nets are needed to make jobs and child care easier. We need to figure out a way to tide people over during true life crises. If lack of time is a major problem, we will need to figure out ways to free up time. Ditto for lack of money.

Coping

There are various ways to cope with stress. That is all well and good, but wouldn't it be nice if there were fewer stresses to have to cope with? Coping is a tool for dealing with stress once it happens.

But let's create a world in which there are fewer stresses and thus less of a need to give our coping skills such a workout. Let's deal with the causes and not the symptoms.

Loss of Self-Reflection

Necessary self-reflection is fading away as life's stresses become greater. Life is not supposed to be one giant coping strategy.

There is a disconnect between what we want and what we are getting. Our wants are sometimes really our needs. If we can reduce stress in our lives, we have a better chance of figuring out what we want out of life and getting our needs met.

Self-Actualization

What has made this world so stressful? What can we do about it? Can we be happier?

I am guessing that most of us would say that we could be happier. To get to a state of greater happiness, we need to reduce the amount of stress in our lives. We need to reduce stress wherever possible to have a chance at a meaningful life. Combating stress is not the point of life. The point of life is to self-actualize in a less stressful environment.

Almost everybody is under some kind of stress, be it from work, family, health, or whatever. But it's causing us to leave our true selves hidden away forever.

Life is about finding our true selves. We need to take care of ourselves to ensure that we are able to lead the lives we are meant to lead. Stress reduction is an important part of self-actualization.

Impact on Politics

In part because we are attending to the stresses in our lives, we let politicians choose candidates for us. We delegate critical decisions to the two-party system. Sure, we can vote, but how did those candidates we vote for get on the ballot? I don't recall selecting them.

Today's political parties reduce the number of candidates to several from their insulated world and then let us vote for one. But I want a real choice. I want the candidates I am voting for to come from a larger pool of people available to me via the Internet, not from a short list in a back room. Let's take our power back and not give it over to career politicians and existing political parties.

Today's two-party candidates are not like us. Let's choose candidates like us so that government is made up of people who see stress reduction as a priority.

Passion for Politics

Participation in politics could be more passionate. What are the possible reasons for this lackluster participation? Lack of time is one. So is a sense of helplessness. People won't participate if they can't make a difference. Let's give people more control over the political process by producing candidates who understand the importance of stress reduction.

Chapter 3

Hurricane Katrina

———————————

Hurricane Katrina is a case in point for the need for a new type of politics. The failed handling of Katrina is evidence of a broken political system. The United States can do much better than that.

Broader Message

In late August 2005, Hurricane Katrina began its unfortunate assault on the United States, focusing its awesome power on New Orleans and other coastal cities. All of us saw the depressing news reports showing the loss of human life and property. But we should also realize that Hurricane Katrina has a broader message about today's broken political system.

Hurricane Katrina outed today's political system as uncompassionate and incompetent. We need to face the fact that our current political system is broken. Going forward, we cannot support leaders like those responsible for the embarrassing response to the suffering in places like New Orleans. We need to adopt a different way of looking at politics to ensure that people like those in charge of the feeble response to Hurricane Katrina are not in leadership roles. Much of the problem stems from today's broken political system, which easily allows uncompassionate and incompetent people to become leaders.

What America needs is a new type of political force, one that will produce leaders who can handle events like Hurricane Katrina with compassion and competence. To get there, we will need to jettison the two-party system that rewards career politicians. In its place, we will need to channel a new kind of political force that makes full use of the Internet.

It is time for the Internet to touch politics. I want to see us use this most modern of technologies to shrink the United States and remake today's politics in the style of old. The Internet can give us the opportunity to participate fully in politics and to shape our destiny. Ultimately, we will select candidates who represent us. These candidates will understand how to respond to crises in a humane way.

Candidates produced through the democracy of the Internet will come from the people. We will be able to harness the power of the Internet to put forth candidates who will understand what to do at a most human level in a crisis.

We will no longer need to rely on the current two-party system to produce candidates. The Internet will allow us to produce candidates who understand life at a different level from the life of insulated privilege that so many current leaders come from.

Pitiful Response

Hurricane Katrina has shown the United States to be in trouble. We have been seen by ourselves and by the rest of the world as ineffectual. Days just kept passing with minimal response from the government. Not enough was done to help relieve the suffering of so many. Although those charged with responding to emergencies may have been ineffectual, the rest of us are not. We must work together to ensure that competent and compassionate people occupy positions of leadership.

Although mighty Hurricane Katrina announced its ominous presence in advance and many were fortunately able to evacuate the threatened areas, many others were unable to leave. Some were too ill to move. Others had no transportation. Illness and poverty interfered with proper evacuation. However, those in power did little to help before the storm came. Would it have hurt to provide buses to help people get out of the affected areas? What were those in charge waiting for?

The government has not meaningfully addressed these failures head on, so we can only guess what, if anything, was going on with our leaders. Racism? Ignorance? An inability to follow weather forecasts? A philosophical opposition to using federal resources to help states? An immature view of the distinction between the private sector and the public sector?

Days passed before many of our citizens received food and water in the wake of the hurricane. News stories highlighted barbaric conditions in the Superdome and in the New Orleans Convention Center. Could all of this be happening in America? Where were the leaders? Murders, rapes, and deaths in the shelters never seemed to sink in with our leadership.

Well, we can do better than this in the future. Let's use the Internet to start a new type of political system that will allow us to select candidates who will respond to disasters in a way that is successful and that doesn't add, through its failures, to our stresses.

Chapter 4

Today's Broken Political System

_____

We need to confront the problems with the current political system. The current political system does not produce representative candidates who reduce our levels of stress. Fortunately, the Internet provides a vehicle for positive political change.

Problems

Once I started pondering the stresses of the modern world, I started thinking about how we can make the world a less stressful place. I see no reason why so many hardworking, decent people have to face so much stress at home, on the job, and elsewhere. I have concluded that much of the problem stems from our broken political system.

Our political system is broken in the sense that politicians are not doing enough to make our lives less stressful. Our stress levels are not being taken into account. We are not being represented. We need to control our destiny. Candidates need to be like us.

The current two-party system is problematic, as is the type of candidate who reaches political office through that system. The political parties are not willing to commit resources to candidates like us. They prefer to back candidates with track records and large bank accounts. Unfortunately, a politician succeeding in today's two-party system is not one of us.

The Reduction of Stress

The current political system is broken and does not address the stresses of the modern world. The current system delegates authority to politicians who use that authority on behalf of corporations, lobbyists, and political cronies.

We need leaders who are regular people. Anyone who has moved up the ranks to become a political candidate today is not a regular person. Too much of politics today is inconsistent with allowing regular people to rise through the ranks.

Our system of government never should have been allowed to devolve to its current state. Fortunately, with the power of the Internet, we have the ability to take the two-party system out of the equation and choose candidates from a variety of backgrounds with a variety of views. The Internet is the force that will allow us to reshape politics in a way that will ultimately reduce our stress levels.

In today's broken political system, the electability of candidates often increases when they play it safe and mislead us about their legislative plans. However, whether a candidate is electable should depend on their experience with, and ability to understand, the stresses of modern life. We shouldn't accept today's system of politics, which produces candidates unlike us.

Politics is now one of the greatest stress producers, as we continually put people unlike us in positions of power. The two-party system is giving us these candidates. Going forward, we need to choose our own candidates from the beginning.

I am proposing to change politics to make it one of the greatest stress relievers. Our stress is reduced when we have control. Using the Internet to choose candidates like us will reduce stress.

We're lucky that the Internet has arrived when it has. We've seen how it has aided us in finding information and in purchasing goods and services. Let's keep using the Internet to buy books and to find information, but let's also harness it for our political needs and for reducing stress.

It's no secret that control reduces stress. If we use the Internet to gain control over our political system and our individual and collective destinies, then we will lead less stressful lives. When we elect candidates who will evaluate the impact of laws and policies on stress, then our stress levels will be reduced.

The Power of the Internet

Our forefathers had a vision of this country that was about representative government. As the country has become larger and more complicated, we have found ourselves devoting our energies to matters other than political participation. That's bad news.

The good news is that it's never too late to change course. Going forward, we need to use the Internet to regain control over the political process. Today's two-party system provides a flawed approach to choosing candidates. The Internet, backed by our renewed engagement in politics, can help individuals take over politics from here on out.

Imagine a world where candidates use the Internet to provide us with information and where we use the Internet to evaluate that information. In that world, regular people will become involved in politics. The job of selecting candidates will move from political parties to individuals.

Once that happens, regular people who experience the stresses of daily life in such areas as jobs, health, divorce, children, and homeownership will run for political office and will offer us a chance to create a world that will value laws and policies built around stress reduction. With the Internet at our disposal, we can run for office ourselves. Let's be part of the group that changes politics for the better via the Internet.

Today's politicians are more likely to represent entrenched corporate interests than to represent regular people. To see a glaring example of this, compare the favorable tax rates facing corporations with the less favorable rates facing individuals. No individual should take this sort of slap in the face sitting down.

Individuals have the right to vote, but corporations don't. This is a nation of individuals, not corporate interests. We need to make sure that we as individuals regain the control that we were always meant to have.

Going forward, the loyalty of our politicians has to be to people and not to entrenched corporate interests and lobbyists. If candidates can reach us via the Internet and if we can choose them via the Internet, then we can bypass the current two-party political process that depends so heavily on large campaign coffers. For candidates to reach people today via television ads, large sums of money are needed. Reaching people via the Internet is open to all.

Choice of Candidates

We can improve the quality of candidates available to us. The type of person who makes it through today's two-party political system is not qualified to lead us. Even those politicians who point to humble backgrounds don't dwell on their current riches.

In the political landscape I envision, those who lead us will be like us and will make decisions that will reduce the stresses of modern life. It's not hard to imagine who will thrive in an environment where real people have a chance of making it to political office. Those who will thrive will be people like us.

Self-actualization, both of ourselves and of our nation, is at stake. To reach our highest state of being, we need a robust political process. A robust political process driven by individuals doesn't have to be a myth. Let's claim politics as the province of each and every person in this country.

The Politics of Old

In a way, the politics of the future is about moving forward while at the same time looking back to a time before big business and special interest groups took politics away from the people. Grafting the Internet onto politics will give us a chance to have political representation that will reduce stress.

Such a vision is both futuristic and nostalgic. Extending the Internet to bring politics back to the individual is futuristic in that it involves a new technology, the Internet. But it is also nostalgic in that it makes the country feel more like a small town. Information that travels around the country with the click of a mouse makes the country seem smaller. As the country feels smaller, it starts to feel more like a small town.

When we ponder the America of old, we notice the ability of any person to rise from humble circumstances to the highest ranks of government. We think of people like Abraham Lincoln, with his folksy charm and keen understanding of human nature. We can elect candidates like that if we as individuals take control of the choice of candidates in this country. We can pick people with the kinds of experiences we value.

The politics of old focused on the individual. The politics of today focuses on corporations and lobbyists. If we use the Internet to force changes in politics, then the politics of the future will again properly focus attention on the individual.

Chapter 5

The Internet

    The Internet has changed many areas of the world. E-commerce is common. E-mail is ubiquitous. Regular folks have Web sites that rival those of corporations. People post and download information constantly. Photographs are posted on the Internet for all to see.

Politics Untouched

As it turns out, the Internet has touched most of the areas of our lives with the major exception of politics. In today's world, we don't vote via the Internet. Candidates reach us primarily via televised debates and ads. If the vision of this book comes to pass, the Internet will become the modern equivalent of the old town hall. The Internet will become the preferred place for politics.

It is time for the Internet to reach politics and to allow us to choose candidates who will advance the agenda of stress reduction. Candidates who currently hide behind unelected handlers and negative television ads will have to stand before us before they are chosen. They will have to play by our rules, not the rules defined by the current two-party political system and the media.

As soon as politics starts to travel on the Information Superhighway, we will be better off.

A New Political Force

Obviously, there is room for a great deal of improvement in politics. We can improve matters via a new kind of political force. This new political force will make full use of the Internet. It is time to bring the Internet to politics.

I want to use the Internet to shrink the United States and remake today's political system in the style of old. The Internet can give us the opportunity to participate fully in politics and shape our destiny. Ultimately, we will be able to select candidates who represent us. These candidates will understand the stresses of modern life and will aim to reduce those stresses.

Step back for a moment and consider what it will mean for you to be able to choose candidates who are like you. A candidate who has lost a job will be more likely to favor legislation to protect us from job loss. A candidate who has been through a divorce will be more likely to understand the needs of people in that situation. The list can go on and on. You should now feel somewhat energized by the prospects of this new vision of politics.

Wouldn't you like to choose politicians who can meet your needs? Politics is about engagement and participation. We never should have turned politics over to career politicians and corporate special interests. Let's take politics back and shape a future that meets our needs and wants.

The Internet Candidate is the vehicle for reshaping our destiny. The Internet Candidate comes from us and is elected by us. As such, the Internet Candidate will make decisions that help people like us, particularly in the area of stress reduction.

Let's wage an Internet revolution in politics. The revolution that results from a move towards the Internet Candidate, who is closer to us and who understands our stress-reduction needs, will change our political landscape for years to come. The full impact of this change in direction won't be felt right away, but it will be felt as soon as our current leaders are replaced by those we have truly chosen.

Our current elected officials are part of the two-party system that is not responsive to the needs of regular people. Let's get rid of the two-party system. Going forward, with the Internet as the backbone, politics will revolve around engagement and participation. We will no longer need political labels to stand in for real ideas.

In the future, the power of the Internet will allow us to give our feedback on a number of issues in real time. If a candidate lies to us, we will be able to express our dissatisfaction directly via the Internet. The true Internet Candidate will appreciate the feedback provided in this way.

Current politicians are satisfied with telephone polls of small numbers of people. Let's show them how the Internet can work. With the Internet, actual feedback can be discerned without the need for extrapolation from limited subsets of data. The vagaries of polling estimates will disappear.

Now is the time to knock the wind out of the sails of the two-party system, special interest groups, corporate lobbyists, expensive campaigns, career politicians, and the like. Let's start a movement that will shock the world. Let's move forward by returning to a simpler time. Let's ensure America's place as the leader of the world.

Chapter 6

The Internet Candidate

The Internet Candidate comes from the people. We should be able to harness the power of the Internet to put forth a candidate who understands the stresses of the modern world and who will work to reduce those stresses. We no longer need to rely on the current two-party system to produce candidates. The Internet will allow us to produce candidates who understand life's stresses and who are committed to reducing those stresses.

The Internet Candidate will be one of us, not just someone fronting the two-party system. We will learn about and choose our candidates through the Internet. The Internet Candidate will be someone who has experienced stress and who understands the importance of making our lives less stressful.

The Internet will allow us to communicate with each other so that we can choose better candidates. It will also allow us to communicate better with political candidates.

Right now, special interest groups dominate politics. We need to use the Internet to make sure that people like us dominate politics. Politics shouldn't be about money and special interests. It should be about quality representation.

We the People

One of the underlying principles of our government is the principle of "We the People," which appears prominently in the preamble to the United States Constitution. Sadly, that principle has been diluted over the years. However, the concept of the Internet Candidate can help us breathe new life into the principle of "We the People".

We can never forget that politics is about representation. Politicians are supposed to represent us, not be foisted upon us. The two-party system foists candidates upon us. Then, we go through the motions of electing politicians from a list of pre-chosen candidates. Thankfully, the Internet Candidate will be chosen directly by us.

The fundamental principles of our government are spelled out to us in grade school. However, these principles have become myths. The principle of "We the

People" is a myth in our current two-party system.

Fortunately, we can resurrect our fundamental principles of government by harnessing the power of the Internet. The Internet has changed business, dating, research, and so forth. Let's use the Internet to change politics, too. What are we waiting for?

Who should the Internet Candidate be? That is up to us. To help alleviate stress in the modern world and create an environment that will allow us to self-actualize, we should choose a candidate who has experienced the stresses of the modern world. The Internet Candidate will allow us to have representative government in the truest sense.

In so many ways, the modern world has left us without a safety net. Such an unfortunate situation means that major life events such as job loss, divorce, or health problems can destroy lives. We need to see the Internet Candidate as an opportunity to create a safety net that will reduce the potential impact of major stressors.

The Internet Candidate will also allow us to move away from party platforms. Some people are conservative fiscally but liberal socially. The two-party system makes it hard for that kind of nuanced candidate to get on the ballot. The Internet Candidate will give us a broader choice. In the new political environment envisioned in this book, leaders can grab the best of the conservative and liberal platforms and offer that up as a realistic alternative.

Elections

In the political landscape defined by the Internet Candidate, the Internet will play a key role before, during, and after elections.

Before an election, candidates will make themselves known via the Internet. Voters will discuss candidates in e-mail and on Web sites. Online polls will take place.

During an election, all voting will be done via the Internet. Results will be presented in real time with complete accuracy. We will no longer require hand counts or worry about chads. Good riddance, chads! No longer will estimates based on a polling of voters substitute for accurate data. The polls will open earlier and close later, making it easier for people who work or take care of children to vote. People will be able to vote from wherever they'd like.

After an election, the Internet will continue to play a key role. Once in office, the Internet Candidate will communicate to people via the Internet. For example, we should be able to view the daily schedules of our leaders. Who are they meeting with? Which city or country are they traveling to? Are they on vacation? Sick? Who is joining them for dinner? What is being served at official dinners? More importantly, the Internet Candidate will solicit input from the electorate to help make decisions. A referendum will be easy and accurate.

In this future state of affairs, Internet access will be critical. The government will need to provide free computers and basic Internet access for those in need so that political participation is available to all.

The Internet allows for the quick dissemination of information. Let's become "We the People" again. Honestly, being "We the Governed" is not the way to go, especially when our leaders are not like us. We complain about the people we elect, but we fail to understand that we as individuals are responsible for electing our representatives. Fortunately, we are not limited to candidates foisted upon us by the two-party system.

Once challenged, those behind the two-party system will fight to preserve the current state of politics. Before the complete dismantling of the two-party system, we should go ahead and vote for the Internet Candidate on the write-in lines on ballots. Backed by the force of the Internet and the widespread desire for participation in government, a write-in candidate could win an election.

Candidates

We need to choose candidates who are like us and who can represent us. To represent us, a candidate needs to have lived through a similar set of stresses. A candidate who has little in common with us will not be an effective representative. We need leaders who have dealt with the stresses of the modern world. The Internet Candidate, chosen by us without reliance on the two-party system, will be able to represent us as we look to government to reduce the stresses in our lives.

As part of this analysis, let's examine the requirements for being president of the United States. There aren't many.

You have to be a citizen by birth who has resided in the United States for at least fourteen years and reached the age of 35. That's pretty much it.

Unfortunately, the two-party system has added some "requirements" that we need to get rid of. For example, successful candidates today have to look presidential and have access to lots of money.

The Internet Candidate can meet the minimal requirements for public office. Access to political parties is not needed.

We need to use the Internet to elect people who will help us change America. America is in need of change. We need to put representatives in office who will help us reduce the stresses of the modern world so that we can go about our lives under as little stress as possible.

Chapter 7

The Stress Index

The Internet will allow us to create a stress index to measure our levels of stress. This index will make the Internet Candidate all the more effective.

Indices

Various indices are available to us right now. Witness the Consumer Price Index and the multitude of stock indices. Notably missing is a stress index to measure our perceptions of stress. To be able to hold politicians accountable for implementing laws and policies that reduce the stresses of modern life, we will need to be able to measure those stresses via a new index that I call the Stress Index.

The Stress Index will allow us to measure our current levels of stress. The Internet will be necessary for this index because this index will have to be current and accurate.

We will be able to provide data for the Stress Index on an ongoing basis. This index will make our leaders accountable for, and responsive to, stress levels in society. Sure, this index is based on perceptions, but perceptions are the most relevant factor in measuring stress.

Measurements

The exact details of the Stress Index do not need to be spelled out right now, but all of us should understand that the Stress Index will consist of questions about various areas of our lives. These questions will need to be answered by many people on an ongoing basis.

What people want out of life might include better health, more money, and more free time, but these are not measured by current indices. The Stress Index will allow us to evaluate how we are doing as a nation in terms of stress. Once we elect leaders who will give us the safety nets and time we need, the Stress Index should show that we are under less stress.

Today's economic indicators do not tell the whole story. Currently, we can read about inflation, the unemployment rate, and the movement of stock prices, but we can't read about the levels of stress in society. The Stress Index will provide visibility to stress levels.

Once we focus on improving our Stress Index scores, we will see an improvement in various areas of human interaction. Once each person's stress level goes down, their interactions with others will be healthier. Those on the receiving end of improved interactions will have less stress in their lives as a result of having fewer toxic interactions. Once this ball starts rolling, we should see constant improvements in our stress levels.

Chapter 8

The Future

_____

The Internet Candidate will ensure that we are represented by people like us who are committed to reducing the stresses in our lives. The Internet Candidate will be readily available to us via the Internet and will take the new Stress Index seriously. Once the Internet

Candidate is the norm, we will see an improvement in our quality of life.

No More Two-Party System

Once the vision of this book is in place, the two-party system will fade away. The two-party system will become irrelevant as we use the Internet to choose candidates. Candidates will communicate directly to us via the Internet instead of indirectly to us via the current political parties. Party primaries will disappear. Backroom meetings to choose candidates will no longer take place. To be a successful candidate in the age of the Internet Candidate, a candidate will have to work directly with people like us.

Online Communication

Once the Internet touches politics, the pressure to move our political system to the online world will be great. Voting and political meetings will take place online. So will communications to and from candidates. Candidates will cheaply and easily communicate with us online. The Internet Candidate, who will be elected by the people and not by the party machinery, will be responsive to us.

The Creation of Community

With the rise of the Internet Candidate, a political community can be created online. The national equivalent of a town meeting can occur. Candidates will be responsive to individuals and will be able to communicate directly with voters. Leaders will be accountable. Our values will be reflected in our leaders.

A Return of Passion

Participation breeds passion. Being able to elect candidates who understand stress and who are committed to reducing it will be critical. When we feel better about our lives and about our role in the political process, we will become more passionate about politics than we currently are. Feelings of helplessness and powerlessness will become a thing of the past. We will be in charge of our destiny.

Chapter 9

Action Items and Challenges

This book is in many ways about changing our mindset so that we can rejoin the political discourse. By focusing on stress reduction through a new kind of political force, we can become engaged in politics. The Internet Candidate who focuses on laws and policies that reduce stress will help individuals self-actualize and will help society become a more fulfilling place.

Action Items

At its core, the call to action is straightforward:

- Read this book, pass it around, and discuss its merits.

- Move away from the current two-party political system.

- Vote for the Internet Candidate, who comes from the people and is responsive to the people. Those who are too jaded, or under too much stress, to participate in politics today will find it easier to participate in this new political landscape, as they can see and feel the impact they can have.

Challenges

One of the largest challenges will be to provide computers and Internet access to everyone. That access is essential for the Internet Candidate to become a reality. The goal is inclusion, not exclusion.

The good news is that cheaper computers and Internet access are being developed as part of a worldwide effort to bring computers and the Internet to poor countries around the world. I am optimistic that something similar can be done in the United States to bring computers and the Internet to everyone. In the meantime, more places for public computing could be set up.

Chapter 10

Conclusion

The stress in today's society is real. As evidenced by the weak response to Hurricane Katrina, the leaders produced by today's broken two-party system are not able to address our needs for stress reduction. In fact, they add to our stress.

Politics is a source of stress, but we can reduce that stress by controlling the selection and election of candidates. We need candidates who are generated by us and not foisted upon us.

With the Internet, we have the opportunity and obligation to fix today's broken political system. The Internet offers us a high-tech way to increase community and get closer to the participatory politics of old.

The Internet Candidate will be a new force for stress reduction. Our needs will be heard and met. A new Stress Index will allow us to measure whether various laws and policies are reducing stress.

If all of us try to improve our lives by electing the Internet Candidate, then we will help ourselves and society as a whole. This book is in some ways about self-help but also about societal change. If the vision of this book comes to pass, we will create a better society.

Let's create a new political world where responsive government results from individual passion. We no longer want politicians to be imposed upon us.

Rather, we would like to choose our representatives from the beginning, not just from the point at which the two-party system hands them to us.

The time has come to fix our broken system of politics. Let's replace the broken system with a better system. The new system, which will result in stress reduction, will be formed around the Internet Candidate, a new kind of political force.

www.ingramcontent.com/pod-product-compliance
Lightning Source LLC
Chambersburg PA
CBHW060955040426
42445CB00011B/1162